FOR HENRY

.

.

.

.

.

.

.

.

.

.

.

.

.

For the sky is not the limit; it is
merely the beginning...

Since Jack was a little boy, he had looked up at the stars, wondering what was out there.

He could remember his beloved Uncle William excitedly pointing out the Big Dipper and the North Star and various planets that came into view on lucky cloudless nights. Jack distinctly remembered looking up at the black sky as a baby and being soothed by the glowing orbs and speckles sparking like glitter.

Now ten years old he had begun to grasp the idea of an infinite universe. On his birthday he was delighted to receive an advanced telescope.

Uncle William pointed it firmly at 360 degrees reminding Jack that if he ever got lost in the night sky, he could always find the North Star from which anyone could navigate their way.

By now Jack didn't need a telescope to identify the North Star: he knew exactly where it was. He gently tilted the telescope lens towards Orion's Belt and across the Milky Way. The galaxy was majestic.

Uncle William was a firm atheist, though he had a childlike hope which brought no end of wonder to Jack's childhood.

William had often told him that shooting stars were not stars at all, but only meteors, nothing more than falling rock-debris crashing through our atmosphere. But if Jack ever did see one, he should make a wish.

"You see," Uncle William would say, "seeing something as unlikely as a shooting star over London is always a reminder of one's own small significance in the universe."

Jane was at work; she couldn't remember ever being this close to dozing off from boredom.

A relentless influx of requests streamed in, each processed with an assigned symbol entirely disregarding the human despair behind it.

As one request after another flooded in, adding to the ever-increasing backlog, Jane couldn't believe she'd spent so long at the organisation, in the same department, doing the same thing every single day.

Full of hope as a young one, Jane had looked upon the movie stars of Hollywood in awe.

What lucky star had they been born under? she often wondered.

But the work had to be done and Jane found herself, nearly twelve years later, still in the same old position at the bureau with very little actually accomplished.

She lent back in her seat, her arms splaying around her. She was about to drearily plod off to the breakroom when she noticed Karen heading that way too.

Karen was the type you avoided at all costs. She would pass some polite and uninterested remark about the weather which would turn into a lengthy dictated conspiracy theory.

"I definitely do not have time for *that* today" Jane thought to herself, and resolved to remain in the peace and quiet at her solitary cocoon.

She went back to processing a batch of requests from a group of students somewhere in Finland.

Jane rarely actually read the requests she was assigned to process, although on especially mind-numbingly dull days she would find one that was humorous.

"I wish I had more money" was usually the one that made her scoff.

"I wish for world peace" made her shudder with a bittersweet chuckle.

How could the dwellers of this exquisitely unique planet be always fighting in the first place?

"Just live in harmony; there's enough natural resources for everyone" she longed to tell them.

How could they not see how lucky they were, with their regenerative resources and flourishing greenery and sea life?

Why couldn't they live wholly contented lives on this singularly flourishing planet?

She'd never be bored on Earth, that's for sure. If only she could get there.

Jack was now twenty years old, travelling across Scandinavia for the next six months on a study trip before returning to his US university.

He'd won a competitive scholarship to study cosmology at the world-renowned California Institute of Technology beginning in the *fall*, as his new chums across the pond would say.

The highlight of Jack's long-planned trip to Northern Europe was reaching Ivalo in Finland, where meteors fell more frequently than Jack had ever seen before.

The Aurora Borealis hadn't disappointed either. As the purples and greens and pinks danced across the night sky, it represented the unwavering fact that the solar flares from the sun were being halted in their path by the earth's protective atmosphere.

Uncle William was always right, he thought, there's no way that science isn't the answer to everything.

Jack and his study group sledged ten miles each day to their chosen point to collect data and ten miles back again.

One day, it occurred to Jack that not one of them used a map.

Not one of them even used a compass.

Jane looked down on Jack. There was one child who'd found his ultimate activity. He was already preoccupied with discovering more and more about such a magnificent planet and the universe. She so enjoyed helping, even from this distance.

The adult Jack looked up from the snow at Polaris in the night sky: with its guidance the students had never lost their way. They knew their path. They had been drawn to it, like an ever-present invisible magnet guiding them in the right direction.

Karen knocked on Jane's cocoon. Jane didn't bother turning around and used her back limbs to open it.

"Any new wars?" asked Karen.

"No," said Jane. "I'm actually helping some child to find his way at the moment."

She couldn't resist saying how. "He's thinking about a trip sometime in his life and I'm just going to slip in a few practical suggestions."

Karen rolled her eyes.

"Predicting what someone light years away will do and sending them messages,"
Karen said wryly.

"I remember when all we did was monitor things, not this stupid helping. Who ultimately gains from this? I have my suspicions..."

But Jane had no time for Karen's conspiracy theories and was already making polite farewell movements with one limb while closing her monitoring cocoon with the others.

She would send the child a message now.

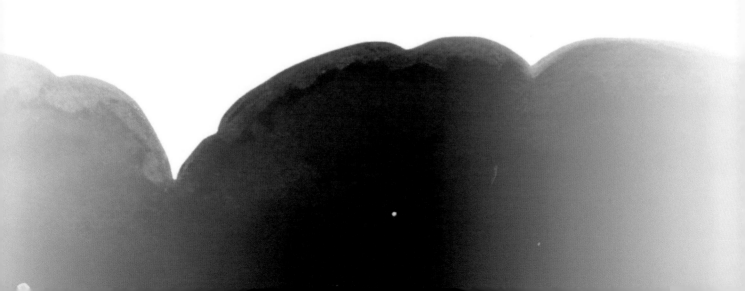

The Department of Hope at the Bureau of Galaxy Assistance hovered approximately nine billion miles above the Earth's sun, right on the outskirts of the Solar System.

Jane's other-worldly technology allowed her compound eyes to detect even the most minuscule detail light years away, from the tiniest bacteria ever-so-slightly warming the polar ice caps on Earth to the last drop of fossil fuel under the Sahara Desert.

Every wish a human on Earth made to the sight of a falling
meteor from space was transmitted to Jane's thought-reading
monitors. The enormous craft, in which Jane sat
alongside many other Guardians, was spectacularly
backlit by a luminescent magnetic bubble.

It was concealed from even the most
exacting telescope by the colossal entity
that Jack and his friends called
Polaris, the North Star.

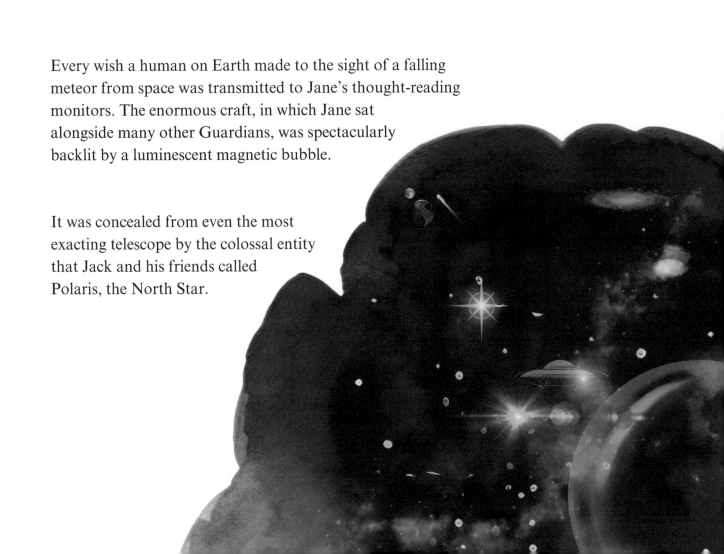

THE END

ASTRA INCLINANT, SED NON OBLIGANT

The stars incline us, they do not bind us

*We are influenced by our destiny, but not
bound by our fate*

REACH FOR THE STARS, AD MELIORA

*"Wonder is the feeling of a philosopher, and
philosophy begins in wonder"*
-Socrates

"Life is an unfoldment, and the further we travel the more truth we can comprehend"
-Hypatia

"Astronomy compels the soul to look upwards and leads us from this world to another"
-Plato

"All truths are easy to understand once they are discovered; the point is to discover them"
-Galileo

"If I have seen further, it is by standing on the shoulders of giants"
-Sir Isaac Newton

*"Humanity will draw more good than evil
from new discoveries"*
-Marie Curie

"We will always have STEM with us. Some things will drop out of the public eye and will go away, but there will always be science, engineering, and technology.
And there will always, always be mathematics"
-Katherine Johnson, NASA

"Our true significance lies in our ability to understand and explore this beautiful universe"
-Professor Brian Cox

"For my part I know nothing with any certainty, but the sight of the stars makes me want to dream"
-Van Gogh

"Not only do we live among the stars,
the stars live within us"
-Dr Neil Degrasse Tyson

"I would rather have questions that can't be answered than answers that can't be questioned"
-Dr Richard P Feynman

"Imagination is more important than knowledge"
-Einstein

"*Don't let anyone rob you of your imagination, your creativity, or your curiosity. It's your place in the world; it's your life.*
Go on and do all you can with it, and make it the life you want to live"
-Astronaut Mae Jemison

"I see the horizon. A light blue, a beautiful band. This is the Earth. How beautiful it is!"
-Astronaut Valentina Tereshkova

"What you do makes a difference, and you have to decide what kind of difference you want to make"
-Dr Jane Goodall

"My dyslexia thinking means I don't just think outside the box, I think outside the planet"
-Dr Maggie Aderin-Pocock DBE

"However difficult life may seem, there is always something you can do and succeed at"
-Professor Stephen Hawking

Printed in Great Britain
by Amazon